10.90

MOROCCO

Keith Lye

Franklin Watts

London   New York   Sydney   Toronto

Facts about Morocco

Area:
446,550 sq. km.
(172,414 sq. miles)

Population:
23,667,000

Capital:
Rabat

Largest cities:
Casablanca (2,409,000)
Rabat-Salé (842,000)
Fez (563,000)
Marrakesh (549,000)

Meknès (487,000)
Oujda (470,000)

Official language:
Arabic

Religion:
Islam

Main exports:
Phosphates, citrus,
fruits, fish

Currency:
Dirham

Franklin Watts
12a Golden Square
London W1

Franklin Watts Inc.
387 Park Avenue South
New York, N.Y. 10016

ISBN: UK Edition 0 86313 646 X
ISBN: US Edition 0 531 10467 2
Library of Congress Catalog Card No:
87-51068

Typeset by Ace Filmsetting Ltd.,
Frome, Somerset
Printed in Hong Kong

© Franklin Watts Limited 1988

Maps: Simon Roulstone
Design: Edward Kinsey
Stamps: Harry Allen International
Philatelic Distributors
Photographs: Barnaby's Picture
Library, 13; GSF Picture Library, 9,
20, 28, 31; Hutchinson Picture Library,
3, 19, 23, 24; Linz, 6; Zefa, 4, 5, 7, 8,
12, 14, 15, 16, 17, 18, 21, 22, 25, 26,
27, 29, 30

Front Cover: Zefa
Back Cover: GSF Picture Library

The Kingdom of Morocco is in the
northwestern corner of Africa. The
city of Tangier is on the north coast,
facing the narrow Strait of
Gibraltar. This strait, which is
between 13 and 37 km (8–23 miles)
wide, separates Morocco from Spain.

High, rugged mountains cover much of Morocco. They are often capped by snow in winter. The Rif Mountains in the north get plenty of rain and contain deep, fertile valleys. Some of the people live in farming villages. Others are nomads.

Morocco's highest peak, Jebel Toubkal, is in the Atlas Mountains. It is 4,165 m (13,665 ft) above sea level. West of the mountains are fertile coastal plains facing the Atlantic Ocean. To the east is the Sahara, the world's biggest desert.

The north coast of Morocco has hot, dry summers and mild, rainy winters. Much of the Atlantic coast gets enough rain for farming, and pleasant sea breezes cool the land. But the southern coastal plains are dry. Agadir in the south has about 25 cm (10 inches) of rain a year.

Some mountain people are nomads, who travel around with their animal herds. Many of them are Berbers, the descendants of early inhabitants of Morocco. Arab armies invaded Morocco in about AD 685. The Arabs introduced their language, Arabic, and their religion, Islam.

Few people live in the dry Sahara,
except at oases where there is water.
In the late 1970s, Morocco took over
the largely desert country of Western
Sahara (formerly Spanish Sahara) to
the south. This country has rich
phosphate deposits. Phosphate is
used to make fertilizers.

Western Sahara covers 266,700 sq km (102,973 sq miles), but it has only about 90,000 people. Some Saharans want independence for their country. They have fought a long war against Moroccan rule. By 1987, Morocco controlled most of Western Sahara, but the war still went on.

The picture shows some of the
money and stamps used in Morocco.
The main unit of currency is the
dirham, which is divided into 100
centimes.

10

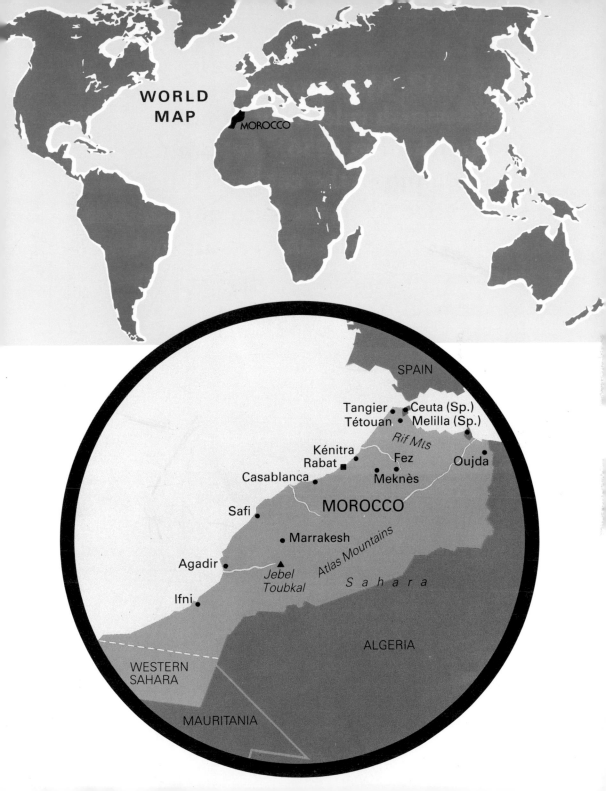

WORLD MAP

MOROCCO

SPAIN

Tangier
Tétouan
Ceuta (Sp.)
Melilla (Sp.)

Rif Mts

Kénitra
Rabat
Fez
Oujda

Casablanca
Meknès

MOROCCO

Safi

Marrakesh

Atlas Mountains

Agadir

*Jebel
Toubkal*

S a h a r a

Ifni

ALGERIA

WESTERN
SAHARA

MAURITANIA

In 1912, Morocco was under French and Spanish rule. It became independent in 1956. Mohammed V, whose tomb in the capital Rabat is shown here, was the king at that time. French and Spanish are still spoken, together with Arabic and various Berber dialects.

Mohammed V Square in Rabat is named after Morocco's former king. He died in 1961 and was succeeded by his son Hassan II as Head of State. The king appoints the prime minister and presides over the cabinet. Morocco has an elected parliament and several political parties.

Casablanca is Morocco's largest
city and chief port. It handles about
three quarters of the country's exports
and imports. About 44 out of every
100 Moroccans live in cities and
towns. Most Moroccans are of Arab
or Berber descent.

Fez is the third largest city after Casablanca and Rabat. The towers that rise in the old part of the city are called minarets. From these towers, muezzins (criers) call Muslims to prayer in the mosques below. About 98 per cent of Moroccans are Muslims.

Marrakesh is the fourth largest city. It has a busy open-air market, which is held in the Djemaa el Fna square. Many kinds of food and craftwork are on sale. Story tellers, acrobats and snake charmers go there to entertain the crowds.

Farmland covers about 17 per cent of Morocco and grazing land another 28 per cent. Morocco is a mainly farming country and agriculture employs 46 per cent of the workforce, as compared with 25 per cent in industry and 29 per cent in services.

Barley, citrus fruits, dates, olives, vegetables and wheat are major crops. Many farmers are poor. They use animals instead of machines to farm the land. Many people use mules or horses for transport.

Citrus fruits are important and Morocco is tenth among the world's top orange producers. Some people, such as the orange sellers seen here, wear western clothes. Others wear hooded cloaks called *djellabiat*.

Morocco has about 14 million sheep and 6 million goats. Wool and leather are used in craft industries. The country has nearly 3 million cattle. They are kept mainly in the lowlands.

Agadir is one of the leading
fishing ports, along with Casablanca
and Safi. Fishing employs about
50,000 workers. They catch anchovies,
sardines and tuna in the sea.

Morocco is known for its carpets.
This picture shows a factory in Fez
where wool is dyed. Other handicrafts
include brasswork, leather goods,
beautiful pottery and tiles, and
various textiles.

Top quality carpets with elegant designs are on sale throughout the country. Many tourists buy them. This display is in a Marrakesh *souk*. Souk is the name for a market or a bazaar.

About 70 per cent of the electricity produced for homes and factories in Morocco comes from hydroelectric stations. Morocco has factories that assemble cars and others that make cement, chemicals, food, metals and soap.

The country's main resource is phosphate ore. Morocco is the world's third leading producer. The picture shows a factory where the ore is processed. Morocco also produces some coal, cobalt, iron, lead, manganese and zinc.

Outside the home, many women still follow the Muslim custom of covering their faces. City people, as here in Rabat, are mostly richer than country people. Because of poverty, Moroccans live, on average, only 59 years. This is 17 years less than people in North America.

Prosperous families encourage their children to work hard at school. Education is now compulsory for children between 7 and 13, but only about a third of Moroccan children go on to secondary schools. Less than three out of every ten Moroccans can read and write.

Food in open-air markets is usually
cheap. A popular food is couscous,
which is made from flour. It is often
eaten with roasted lamb or chicken
and vegetables. Hot tea with mint is
a common drink.

Musicians create exciting rhythms for dancers by beating drums or clapping their hands. Major pastimes include hunting and river fishing, together with such sports as basketball, soccer and swimming.

Many Moroccans are superb riders. In particular, Berber riders give spectacular displays, including mock battles. Berber nomads still depend on their horses in order to travel around the country.

Moroccans are working hard to raise their living standards. But Morocco faces many problems, such as poverty in country areas, which is made worse by droughts. The population is also increasing quickly, while the war in Western Sahara has been extremely costly.

Index